ROBERT FULTON
AMERICAN INVENTOR

William Morrison

INFOMAX
COMMON CORE
READERS

Rosen
Classroom™

New York

Published in 2014 by The Rosen Publishing Group, Inc.
29 East 21st Street, New York, NY 10010

Book Design: Michael J. Flynn

Photo Credits: Cover Stock Montage/Archive Photos/Getty Images; pp. 3, 4, 6, 8–10, 12, 14, 16, 18, 20, 22–24
(background) Apostrophe/Shutterstock.com; p. 5 courtesy of the Library of Congress; p. 7 (Robert Fulton) DEA PICTURE
LIBRARY/De Agostini Picture Library/Getty Images; p. 7 (brooch) DEA/A. DAGLI ORTI/De Agostini Picture Library/
Getty Images; pp. 9 (painting), 13 Science & Society Picture Library/SSPL/Getty Images; p. 9 (frame) Rufous/
Shutterstock.com; p. 11 Encyclopaedia Britannica/Universal Images Group/Getty Images; p. 15 FPG/Archive Photos/
Getty Images; p. 17 Universal Images Group/Getty Images; p. 19 SuperStock/Getty Images; p. 21 nikitsin.smugmug.com/
Shutterstock.com.

ISBN: 978-1-4777-2649-5
6-pack ISBN: 978-1-4777-2650-1

Manufactured in the United States of America

CPSIA Compliance Information: Batch #CS13RC: For further information contact Rosen Publishing, New York, New York at 1-800-237-9932.

Contents

Steamboat Inventor

Robert Fulton was a great inventor whose steamboat **design** changed American life in the 1800s. While Fulton didn't invent the steamboat, he invented the first steamboat to be **commercially** successful. He also had many important ideas about water travel.

Fulton's parents were Irish immigrants, or people who moved from Ireland to America. His father was a farmer, but he couldn't make enough money to keep the farm. When Fulton was young, his family lost the farm, and his father died.

Robert Fulton was born in Lancaster County, Pennsylvania, on November 14, 1765.

Early Life

Fulton's family didn't have a lot of money. He grew up in the countryside of Pennsylvania and learned to read and write at home. When he was 8, he was sent to school to learn more.

Like many young men in the 1700s, Fulton was sent to a business to be an apprentice. Apprentices worked for no money, but they learned a skill that would help them in the future. When he was only 17, Fulton was sent to Philadelphia to work in a **jewelry** store.

At the jewelry store, Fulton painted tiny pictures on jewelry, such as necklaces and rings. This jewelry was popular in the late 1700s.

Robert Fulton

A Great Painter

Fulton became a great painter while working at the jewelry shop. He used the money he earned from painting to buy his mother a farm. Then he went back to Philadelphia to work more on his painting skills.

At this time, some people were trying to improve the arts in Philadelphia. Local **merchants** decided to give Fulton an opportunity to grow as a painter. They paid for him to go to London, England, to learn from great painters there. Unfortunately, Fulton's paintings were skillful, but they didn't earn him very much money.

Robert Fulton was very good at painting portraits, like this one. Unfortunately, painting made him very little money.

Water Transportation

Fulton discovered a new interest: **transporting** goods by water. In 1787, American inventor John Fitch built a boat with a steam engine, or a steamboat. It wasn't commercially successful, but it showed great progress for water transportation. Transporting goods and people by water, safely and quickly, was becoming a possibility.

Up until this point, goods were carried on sailboats called sloops. They were slow, and their speed depended on the wind. A successful steamboat would make it possible to transport goods more quickly.

Steamboats run on steam engines. Steam is made when heated water turns to gas. It creates pressure in the engine, which powers the parts that move the boat forward.

Fulton did some experiments with steamboat design. He started to invent new steamboats that would be better for travel. He also had ideas about canals. Canals are man-made waterways that connect inland towns to major shipping routes. A successful system of canals would increase trade by making it easier to transport goods all over the country.

Fulton wrote plans for a system of canals in a book, which was **published** in 1796. It included important reasons why canals should be built.

Not many people took Fulton's canal ideas seriously, but he continued to create new ideas for shipping.

13

A New Design

Fulton also designed warships and submarines for both France and England, but none of them were successful. In 1801, just when he seemed to be failing as an inventor, he met Robert R. Livingston.

Livingston was an important person in the steamboat business in the United States. Fulton's newest steamboat designs interested him, and soon they became business partners. They both found money to pay to have Fulton's steamboat built. The steamboat would be 66 feet (20 m) long and have side paddlewheels and a strong engine.

Robert R. Livingston

The first steamboat design didn't work, but Livingston was Fulton's partner through failure and success. Fulton even married Livingston's niece, Harriet!

15

In 1806, Fulton's improved designs were made into a real steamboat. It was built in New York City and was 150 feet (46 m) long! It had a paddlewheel on each side and ran on a powerful steam engine.

In 1807, Fulton's steamboat was ready to be tested. It traveled on the Hudson River from New York City to Albany, a distance of about 150 miles (240 km). It took other boats almost four days to make that journey, but it took Fulton's steamboat only 32 hours!

Fulton's boat traveled almost 5 miles (8 km) an hour. It was seen as a great success!

17

The Clermont

Fulton continued to improve his steamboat. He added cabins so people could be more comfortable while traveling. He put short walls around the deck, so people couldn't fall off the boat and so others wouldn't attack it. Every two weeks, Fulton's boat traveled between New York City and Albany three times, carrying people and goods.

In 1808, Fulton's boat was officially called the *North River Steamboat of Clermont*, or *Clermont* for short. Unlike other steamboats, *Clermont* made a lot of money and was successful in transporting people and goods.

This painting shows Robert Fulton's *Clermont* being used to transport people. It was a great success!

In his last years, Fulton continued improving water transportation. In 1812, he was part of a group that pushed to have the Erie Canal built, which improved shipping in New York. Soon after the *Clermont* success, hundreds of steamboats were built and used on many U.S. waterways. Steamboats became easy, fast ways to travel and trade.

Fulton died on February 24, 1815. In his life, he improved the ways Americans traveled and explored the country. Called the "father of the steamboat" by some, Fulton designed inventions that greatly changed American life.

Steamboats along the Mississippi River became an important part of life there, and trips often included music and fun.

Robert Fulton's Life

1765
Fulton is born.

1787
Fulton moves to London to study painting.

1796
Fulton publishes his book on canals.

1801
Fulton meets Robert R. Livingston.

1806
The *Clermont* is built in New York City.

1807
The *Clermont* has a successful test run on the Hudson River.

1811
Fulton's *New Orleans* is the first steamboat to travel in western waters.

1812
Fulton is part of a group that pushes to have the Erie Canal built.

1815
Fulton dies.

Glossary

commercial (kuh-MUHR-shuhl) Having to do with making money.

design (dih-ZYN) A plan or outline showing how something is to be built.

jewelry (JOOL-ree) Rings, watches, necklaces, and other pretty things worn on the body.

merchant (MUHR-chuhnt) One who buys goods and sells them to make money.

publish (PUH-blish) To prepare and sell something for the public to read or use.

transport (TRANS-pohrt) To carry from one place to another.

Index